All-in-One

Step by Step
by
Edna Mae Burnam

Lessons • Theory • Solos

PLAYBACK+
Speed • Pitch • Balance • Loop

The exclusive **PLAYBACK+** feature allows tempo changes without altering the pitch.
Loop points can also be set for repetition of tricky measures.

To access audio visit:
www.halleonard.com/mylibrary

Enter Code
7551-3833-8650-9176

ISBN 978-1-4950-6123-3

EXCLUSIVELY DISTRIBUTED BY

HAL•LEONARD®
CORPORATION
7777 W. BLUEMOUND RD. P.O. BOX 13819
MILWAUKEE, WISCONSIN 53213

Visit Hal Leonard Online at
www.halleonard.com

PREFACE

My aim and purpose in presenting *Step by Step* is a sincere hope that it will help every student become aware of the joy that comes in being able to express themselves musically.

Step by Step will help make learning to play the piano a happy and joyous experience.

Step by Step presents the rudiments of music in a logical order, with gradual and steady progress, presenting a challenge toward increasing pianistic facility.

Step by Step provides appealing, melodious music for the student to play and it keeps this music within the range of the student's ability thereby enabling fluent and artistic performance.

Step by Step further stimulates the student's interest by containing written work in the form of "musical games," thereby giving theory an exciting approach.

Step by Step will help to awaken a deep love for music – the rightful heritage of all.

EDNA MAE BURNAM

CONTENTS

NOTE: Edna Mae Burnam wrote *Pieces to Play* in 1978 and *Write It Right* in 1979, performance and theory books intended as learning enhancements to the *Step by Step* method (1959). She carefully indicated when and where each new performance piece and theory exercise should be studied, and this All-in-One edition features each of the supplementary solos and worksheets located where Burnam intended them to be.

TO THE TEACHER

Edna Mae Burnam's *Step by Step All-in-One Piano Course* is designed to present to the beginning piano student the many subjects they must learn in order to be able to read and play music.

If these subjects are presented too quickly, or too many given at one time, confusion and a distaste for music may result.

This book presents these subjects in their logical order and ONE AT A TIME. Sufficient work is given at each step so that the student will thoroughly comprehend a topic before going on to the next one.

In Book 1, as with those that follow, the subjects dealt with are covered in a clear and complete manner. The musical exercises lie under the hands, and music writing games add to musical knowledge. In addition, theory exercises from *Write It Right Book 1* and performance pieces from *Pieces to Play Book 1* have been incorporated. A final check-up and review ensures complete understanding.

When *Step by Step All-in-One* is completed, the student will have learned the following:

1. How the fingers are numbered for piano playing.

2. Learn to recognize and name the following rudiments:

   Treble clef
   Bass clef
   Brace
   Grand staff
   Bar line
   Measure
   Double bar
   Finger markings (fingerings)

3. Learn to name and play the following notes:

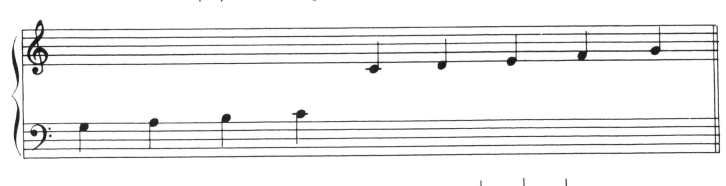

4. Learn the number of counts for the following kinds of notes: ♩   ♩   ♩.   𝅝

5. Learn the number of counts for the following kinds of rests:

6. Learn to play and count in the following time signatures: **2/4**   **3/4**   **4/4**

7. Learn to play and count a tie correctly.

THIS IS HOW YOU NUMBER YOUR FINGERS
FOR PLAYING THE PIANO

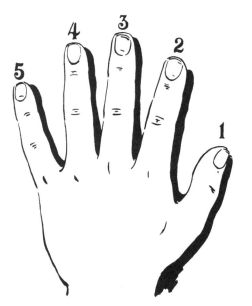

Left hand   **Right hand**

HERE ARE TWO BLACK KEYS

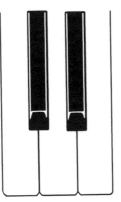

Find them on the piano.

See how many groups of the two black keys you can find.

Play them one at a time and sing "One, Two."

Use any fingers you wish.

MIDDLE C ON KEYBOARD

Find the WHITE note to the left of the two black keys (in the **middle** of the keyboard).

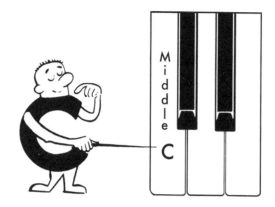

This WHITE note is named MIDDLE C.

Play it with either hand but use your FIRST finger (thumb) as you play MIDDLE C.
Sing C as you play it.

TREBLE CLEF

This is a **treble clef** sign

Notes from MIDDLE C to the **top** of the keyboard to the **right,** are written **after** a treble clef sign.

BASS CLEF

This is a **bass clef sign**

Notes from MIDDLE C to the **bottom** of the keyboard to the **left,** are written **after** a bass clef sign.

MIDDLE C's PLAY YARD

MIDDLE C has a wide yard to play in.

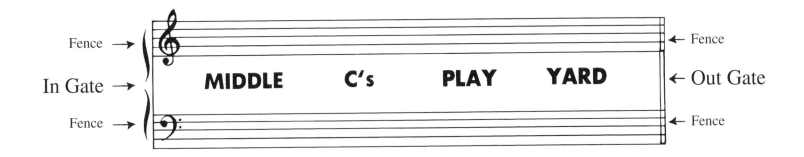

There is a fence on two sides of the play yard.

There is a fancy iron gate to go *into* the play yard.

There is a double bar iron gate at the end of the play yard.

MIDDLE C *never* goes out of the play yard.

PICTURES OF MIDDLE C

MIDDLE C is **always in** the play yard. It may be in different parts of the play yard but it cannot climb on the fences.

MIDDLE C **always** has a line going through it ———▸ ⊕   (this is called a **leger** line).

Sometimes MIDDLE C has a stem.

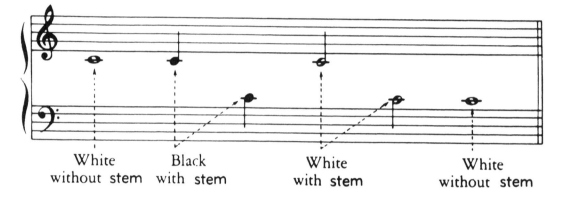

The stem may point up ⊕ or it may point down ⊖

MIDDLE C may be white ⊕ or it may be black ●

Look below and see the different pictures of MIDDLE C in the play yard.

| White without stem | Black with stem | White with stem | White without stem |

LOOK AT THE PICTURES OF MIDDLE C

Play MIDDLE C just as many times as you see it in the play yard.

Use either hand you wish, but use your **first** finger (thumb).

Begin at the "In Gate" and play each MIDDLE C to the "Out Gate".

Keep your eyes on the MIDDLE C's so that you will not lose your place!

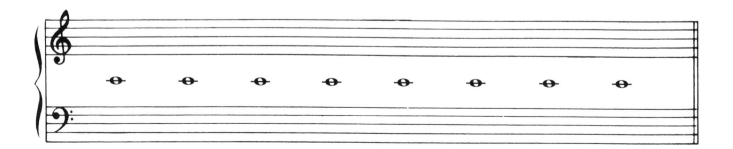

Here is a picture of MIDDLE C with a stem pointing **up** ⟶

Is the stem on the right or left side of MIDDLE C?

When the stem goes **up,** you must play MIDDLE C with the hand that is on the same **side** as the stem. (Your **right** hand).

Use the **first** finger (thumb) of your **right** hand as you play the MIDDLE C's below.

The number 1 above MIDDLE C is a finger mark. It means to use the first finger of your right hand.

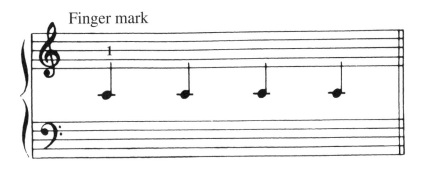

When the stem goes **down** you must play MIDDLE C with the hand that is on the same side as the stem (your **left** hand).

Use the **first** finger (thumb) of your **left** hand as you play the MIDDLE C's below.

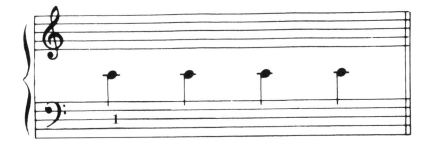

HERE ARE MORE MIDDLE C's

Be sure you play each C with the correct hand!

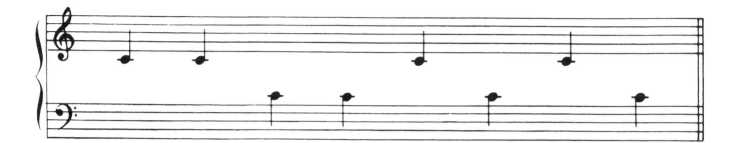

COUNT THREE KINDS OF MIDDLE C's

When Middle C is **black** and has a stem, it sings long enough for you to count **ONE**. (This is a **quarter** note.)

Play and count 1

When Middle C is **white** and has a stem, it sings a little longer. Long enough for you to count **ONE, TWO**. (This is a **half** note.)

Play and count 1, 2

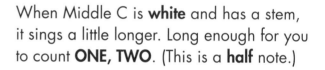
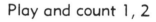
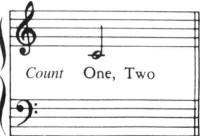

When Middle C is white and has **no** stem, it sings even longer. Long enough for you to count **ONE, TWO, THREE, FOUR**. (This is a **whole** note.)

Play and count 1, 2, 3, 4

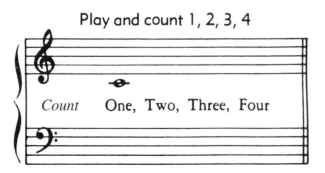

BAR LINES – DOUBLE BAR LINES – MEASURES

There are lines separating MIDDLE C's play yard. In music, these are called **bar lines**.

The places **between** these bar lines are called **measures**.

Notice the last heavy **double bar**. It means we have come to the end.

How many measures are there below?

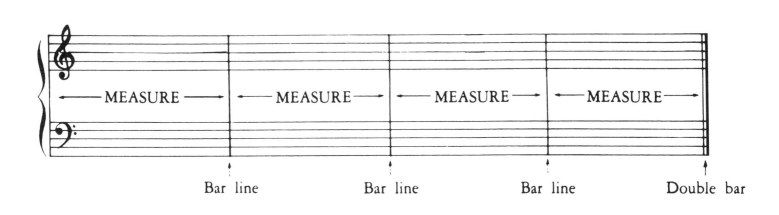

BRACE – STAFF – GRAND STAFF

The music name for "fence" is **staff**. The staff is made up of **lines** and **spaces**.

This is a **brace.**
It holds the treble and bass staffs together and forms a **grand staff** so that we can read notes from the entire keyboard.

Here are the **lines**.

The places between are called **spaces**.

Usually the right hand plays notes written on the treble staff.

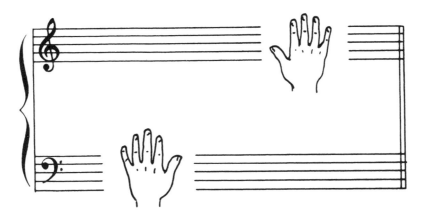

Usually the left hand plays notes written on the bass staff.

$\frac{2}{4}$ TIME SIGNATURE

Notice the numbers on the fences.

You must remember the one that is on **top.**

What is it?

It means that you must count 1, 2 in **every measure.**

These numbers are called TIME SIGNATURES.

After every **bar** line you must **always** begin counting ONE again.

Clap and **count** for each MIDDLE C below.

Do not stop until you reach the **double bar** at the end.

1/2 **TIP TOE**

Count like this One, Two, One, Two, One, Two, One, Two.

Did you remember to count, ONE, TWO in the last measure?

Now **play** and count. Use correct hands and fingers.

The name of this piece is TIP TOE.

When you can **play** and **count** this piece perfectly, you may sing these words:—

"Tip - toe, Tip - toe, Here I Go".

Now play TIP TOE again and your teacher will play with you.

Teacher's Part

$\frac{4}{4}$ TIME SIGNATURE

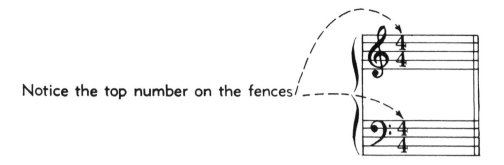

Notice the top number on the fences!

This means that you must count 1, 2, 3, 4 in every measure.

Clap and count the piece named HOP and STOP.

When you can play and count it perfectly you may sing the words.

3/4

HOP and STOP

Hop and stop. Hop and stop. Hop and hop and stop.

Teacher's Part

Here is another piece for you to learn in the same way.

5/6

POP CORN

Come and have some Pop Corn, Snow white pop-ping Pop Corn.

Teacher's Part

D ON KEYBOARD

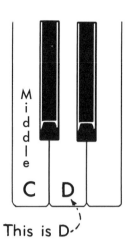

Find the next note to the **right** of Middle C (**between** the two black keys).

This is D

Play D with the **second** finger of your **right** hand.
Sing D as you play it.

Here are some pictures of D.

Remember that D is the note **between** the two black keys.
D does **NOT** have a leger line through it.
D is in Middle C's play yard. It can only play in the **top** of the play yard.
Use the second finger of your right hand to play D.

Here are some pieces for you to play:

SLEEP

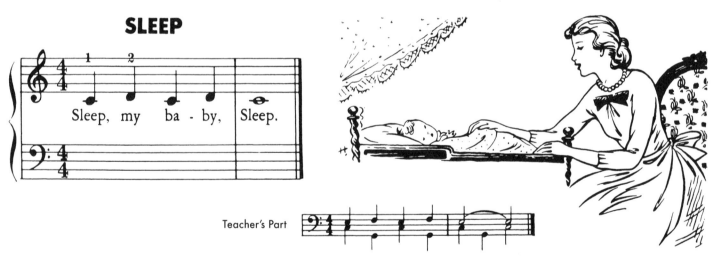

Sleep, my ba - by, Sleep.

Teacher's Part

7/8

ON THE BUS

On the bus the peo - ple trav - el, All a - round the town.

Teacher's Part

THE RAIN

9/10

Hear the gen - tle rain, On the wind - ow - pane.

Teacher's Part

LEAVES

11/12

Leaves are fall - ing down, All a - round the town.

Teacher's Part

Write the right letter name on the key for every **C** and **D** on this keyboard.

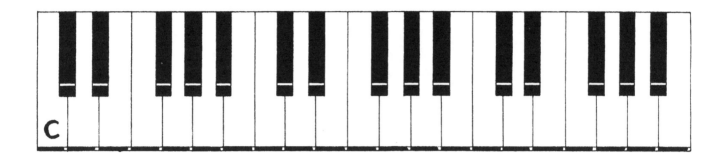

COOKIE JARS

The notes on each cookie jar tell how many cookies are inside.
Write the right number of cookies **(counts)** in the box under each cookie jar.
If you get the right answer for all of them, you will receive a cookie.

ARCHERY

Draw a long arrow from each **term**

to the right sign on the target.

BASS CLEF

TIME SIGNATURE

TREBLE CLEF

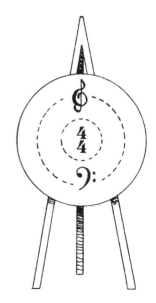

A LETTER

Here is a letter.
Write the right name of each **note** in the box by the note.
If you get the right answer for all of them, the letter will be for you!

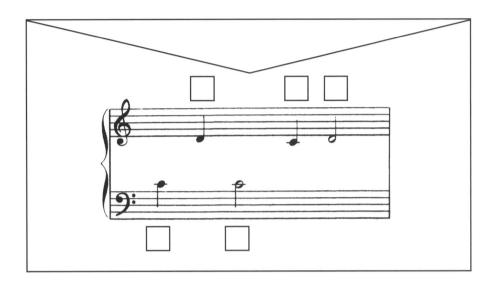

QUESTIONS

What is the name
of this note?   _____

How many counts
does this note receive?   _____

How many counts are in each
measure for this time signature?   _____

Which hand plays when
the stem goes up?   _____

What does a double bar mean?   _____

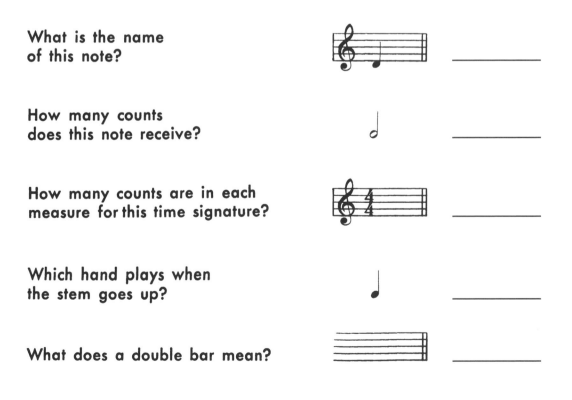

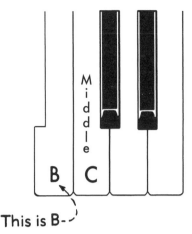

Find the white note
to the **left** of Middle C.

This is B--

Play B with the **second** finger of your **left** hand.

Sing B as you play it.

PICTURES OF B

Here are some pictures of B.

B is in Middle C's play yard. It can only play in the **bottom** of it.

Use the second finger of your **left** hand as you play B.

Here are some new pieces for you to play.

BOAT SONG

Rock my lit - tle boat.

Teacher's Part

13/14

THE DRUM

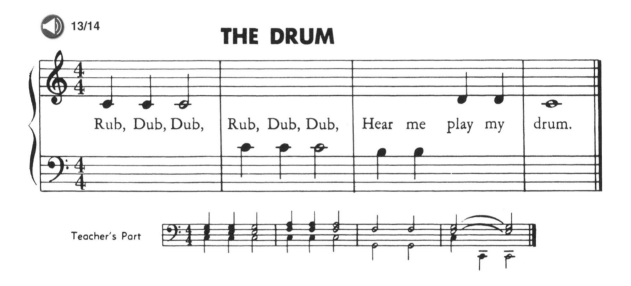

Rub, Dub, Dub, Rub, Dub, Dub, Hear me play my drum.

Teacher's Part

15/16

IN A HAMMOCK

Back and forth, and back and forth, and back and forth, I'm swing-ing.

Teacher's Part

Here is a piece named THE WOODPECKER

Notice the third measure.

In this measure the **right** hand plays on counts 1, 2, 3, 4.

The **left** hand plays on counts 1, 2, 3, 4 **also.**

You must play with **both hands at the same time** in this third measure!

THE WOODPECKER

17/18

Tap, tap, tap, tap.   Tap, tap, tap, tap.   Tap - ping all day long.

Teacher's Part

Write the right letter name on the key for every **B, C,** and **D** on this keybooard.

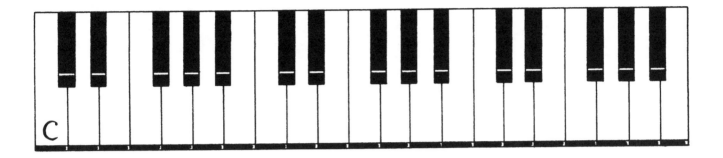

BAR LINES

This line of notes needs **bar lines.**
Draw in **bar lines** in the right places, and put a **double bar** at the end.

$\frac{2}{4}$ ♩ ♩ ♩ ♩ ♩ ♩ ♩ ♩ ♩ ♩ ♩ ♩ ♩ ♩

HOUSES

The **notes** on each house tell how many people live in the house.
On the chimney of each house, write the right number of people to be found inside.

WRITE IT RIGHT
Lesson 2, cont.

JIGSAW PUZZLES

Draw a line from each piece of a puzzle in column **One** to the matching half in column **Two.**

One   **Two**

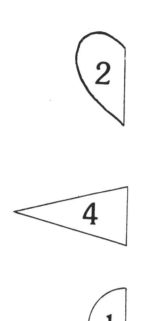

QUESTIONS

What is the name
of this note?    _____

How many counts does
this note receive?   𝅗𝅥 _____

How many counts are in
each measure for this
time signature?   _____

Which hand plays when
the stem goes down?   _____

What is the name of this sign?   _____

E ON KEYBOARD

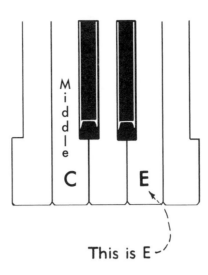

Find the white note
to the **right** of D.

This is E

Play E with the **third** finger of your **right** hand.

Sing E as you play it.

PICTURES OF E

Here are some pictures of E

E is **not** in MIDDLE C's play yard. It is on the **treble** staff.

How many lines make up the treble staff?

E is on the treble staff — on **this** line. _ _ _ _ _ _

Play E with the **third finger** of your **right hand.**

Sing E as you play it. Here are some pieces for you to play.

Remember the numbers
on the fences!

The **top** one is the one
you must remember!

Count 1, 2 in every
measure!

🔊 19/20

SING TO ME

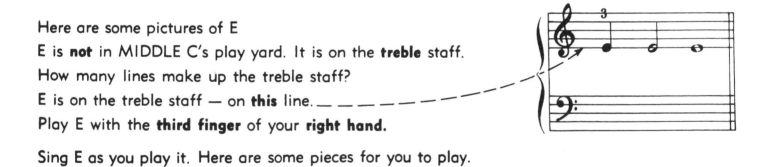

Sing   to   me,   C   D   E.

Teacher's
Part

Here are more pieces for you to play.

THE SHOE COBBLER

21/22

Rap, tap, tap, tap, | Rap, tap, tap, tap, | Cob-bler mend my | shoe.

Teacher's Part

23/24

THE RAIN

Pit-ter, pat-ter, | goes the rain,

On the birds and | flowers. | Pit-ter, pat-ter, | goes the rain, | For so man-y | hours.

Teacher's Part

MARCH OF THE RADISHES

25/26

BY EDNA MAE BURNAM

Moderately fast
Steady and firm

medium loud

Hold these notes
a little longer.

Hold these notes
a little longer.

A ON KEYBOARD

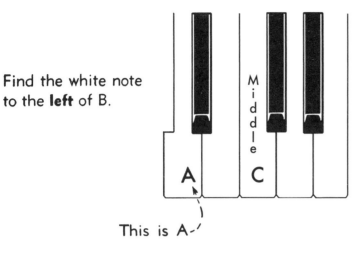

Find the white note
to the **left** of B.

This is A

Play A with the **third** finger of your **left** hand.

Sing A as you play it.

Here are some pictures of A.

A is **not** in MIDDLE C's play yard. It is on the **bass** staff.

How many lines make up the **bass** staff?

A is on the bass staff — on **this** line.

Play A with the **third** finger of your **left hand.**

Sing A as you play it.

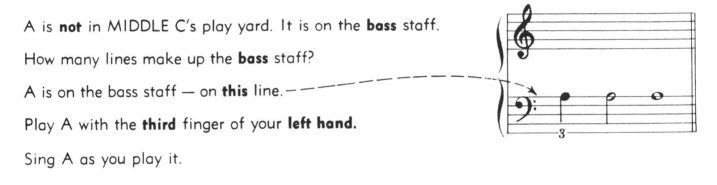

KITTY CAT

Kit - ty cat is sleep - ing. Sleep-ing in the sun.

Teacher's Part

IN THE SNOW

Down I go, In the snow.

Teacher's Part

TWO SINGING

Right hand is Mother's voice.
Left hand is Father's voice.

Moth - er sings and Dad - dy sings, and now they sing to - geth - er.

Teacher's Part

A LONELY TUNNEL

33/34

BY EDNA MAE BURNAM

Moderately slow
Sad and lonely

medium soft

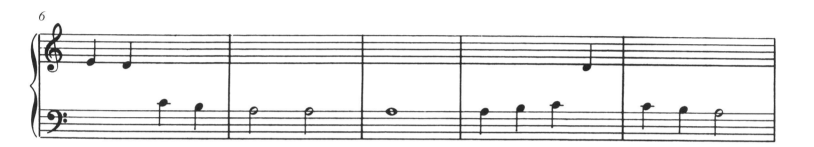

Hold these
notes a little
longer.

very soft

Here is the **grand staff** (both treble and bass staff).

1) Number the **lines** in the treble staff.
2) Number the **spaces** in the treble staff.
3) Number the **lines** in the bass staff.
4) Number the **spaces** in the bass staff.

Treble clef

Brace

Bass clef

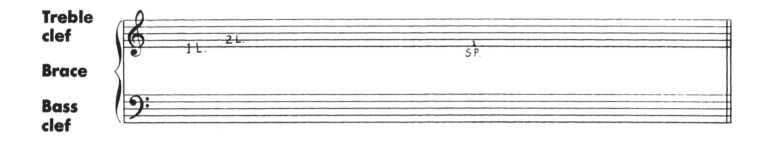

MAIL BOX

There are four **notes** in this mail box.
Write the letter name of **each note** in the box by the note.
If you get all of them right, you will receive four notes in the mail.

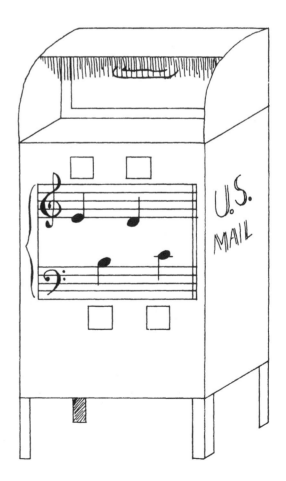

DRUM BEATS

Write in the right **time signature** for this line of drum beats.

QUESTIONS

How many lines are in the **treble staff?** _____

How many lines are in the **bass staff?** _____

How many spaces are in the **treble staff?** _____

How many spaces are in the **bass staff?** _____

What is the name of this **note?** _____

What line is this note on in the **treble staff?** _____

CROSSING THE CREEK

Here is a little creek. Each circle is a rock. Write the name of each note in the circle.

See if you can cross the creek without getting your feet wet!

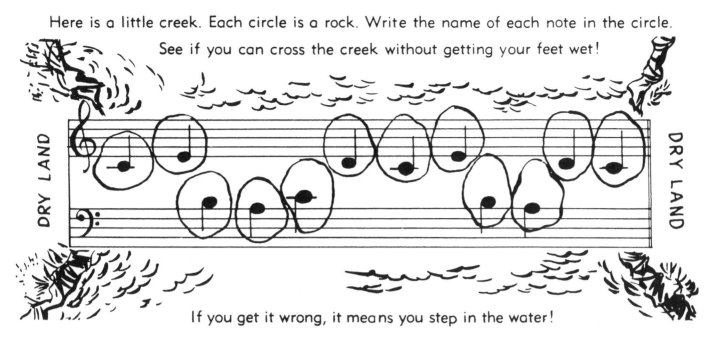

If you get it wrong, it means you step in the water!

BIRTHDAY CAKES

Here are birthday cakes that need candles.

Put as many candles on each cake as there are **counts** in the **notes** on the cake.

A note like this ♩ gets **one** count.   The first one is done to show you how to do the others.

SOLDIERS

Each soldier beats **four measures** on his drum.

The soldier is beating either $\frac{2}{4}$ or $\frac{4}{4}$ time.

Write the **time signature** before each line.

Write the **counts** under each note. Like this

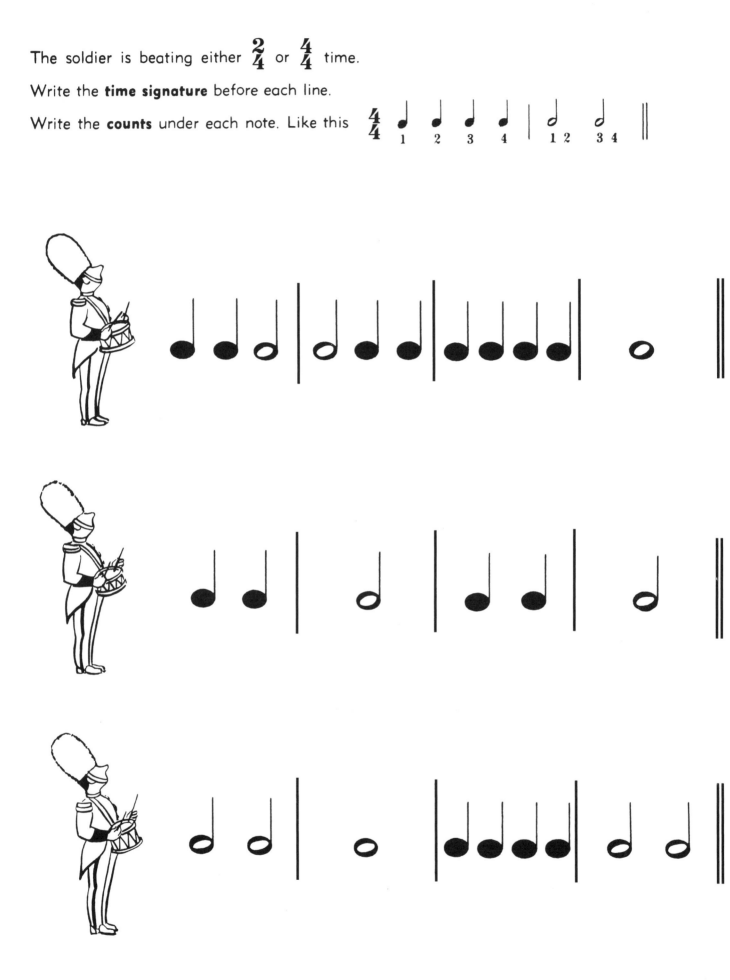

$\frac{3}{4}$ TIME SIGNATURE

You have had pieces
with **two** counts in a measure.

You have had pieces with
four counts in a measure.

Notice the **top**
number in this
time signature.

This means that you
must count 1, 2, 3 in
each measure.

One, Two, Three

You know that a note like this ♩ sings long enough for you to count 1, 2.

When a note like this has a dot after it ♩· it sings long enough for you to count 1, 2, 3.

Here are some pieces for you to play.

NORTH WIND

35/36

North wind is blow-ing and sing-ing a song.

Did you remember to count 1, 2, 3 for
the last note?

Teacher's Part

SWIMMING POOL 37/38

Swim-ming a - round in a swim-ming pool,

Swim-ming a - round keeps me nice and cool.

Teacher's Part

ICE CREAM CONE 39/40

I'd like an ice cream cone. Straw-ber-ry ice cream cone.

Teacher's Part

HOT CROSS BUNS 41/42

Hot Cross Buns, Hot Cross Buns! One a pen-ny, Two a pen-ny, Hot Cross Buns!

Write the right letter name on the key for every **A, B, C, D** and **E** on this keyboard.

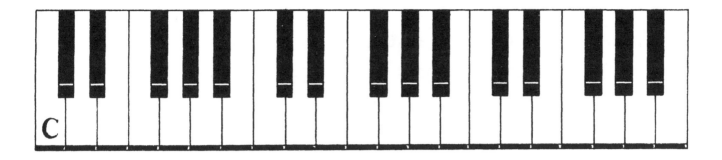

TIME SIGNATURES

Here are three **time signatures.**
Write in the boxes the right number of **counts per measure**
that each time signature tells.

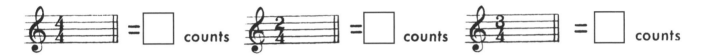

PHONES

The note under each phone tells how many rings (counts) it receives for a call.
Write the right number of rings for each phone in the box under the note.

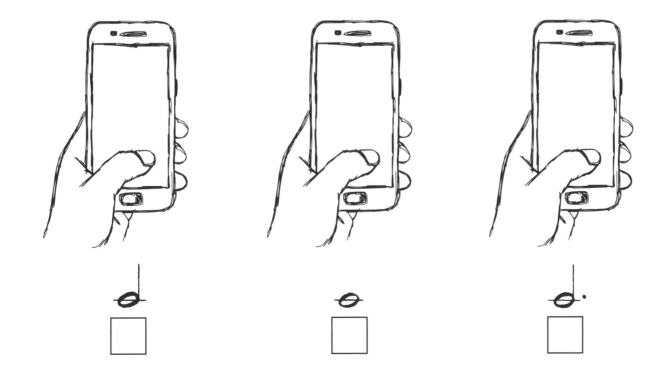

NAMES OF NOTES

Write the right **letter name** of each note in the box by the note.

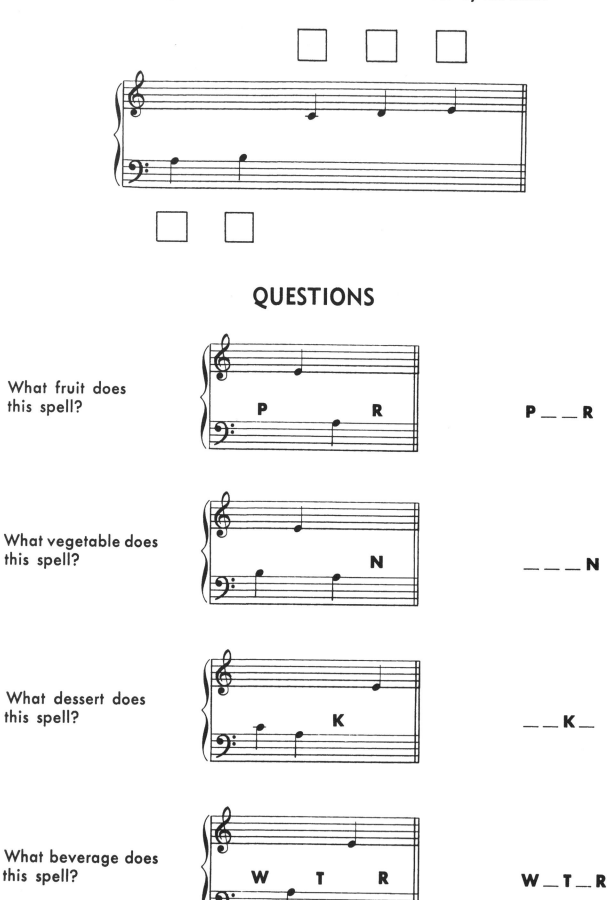

QUESTIONS

What fruit does
this spell?

P _ _ R

What vegetable does
this spell?

_ _ _ N

What dessert does
this spell?

_ _ K _

What beverage does
this spell?

W _ T _ R

SOFT SHADOWS

43/44

BY EDNA MAE BURNAM

Moderately fast

softly

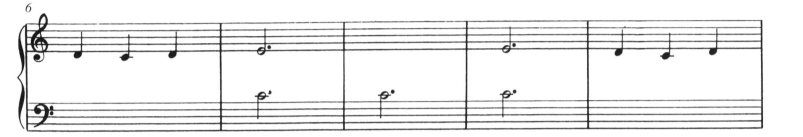

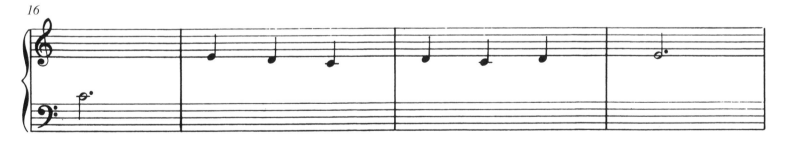

a little slower

Hold these notes
a little longer.

A TIE

When the same note is pictured **two** times, and they are **tied together** with a curved line like

this ♩‿♩ or ◡ this is called a **tie.**

When this happens you must play the **first** note, and **HOLD** the second note and **count** it.

DO NOT LIFT YOUR HAND AND PLAY THE SECOND (or tied) NOTE AGAIN.

Here are some **ties.**

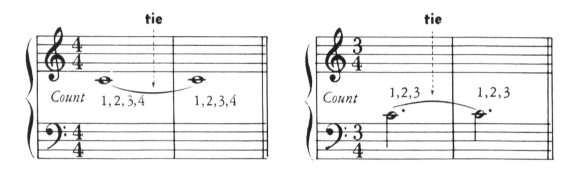

Here are some pieces with **ties.** Point them out.

BOSSY COW

45/46

Boss - y | Cow sings, | "Moo, ___ | I have | milk for | you."

Point out the **ties** in the Teacher's part.

Teacher's
Part

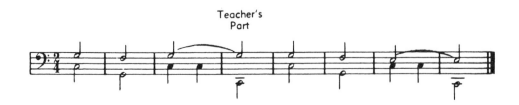

GOLDFISH

Gold-fish swim a - round, and round, and round.

Gold-fish nev - er, nev - er make a sound.

Teacher's
Part

SNOWY WHITE CLOUDS

49/50

Snow - y white clouds in the sky,— Sail - ing by.

Teacher's
Part

WRITE IT RIGHT
Lesson 5

TIED NOTES

Write the right number of **counts** needed in each box.

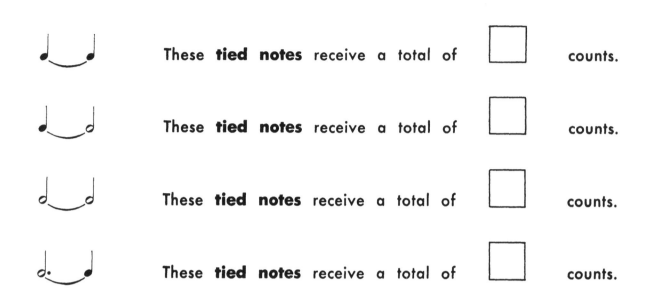

These **tied notes** receive a total of ☐ counts.

These **tied notes** receive a total of ☐ counts.

These **tied notes** receive a total of ☐ counts.

These **tied notes** receive a total of ☐ counts.

FISHING

Each **note** is a fish.
Write the right **letter name** of each note in the box by the note.
The fisherman will catch every fish (note) that you name correctly.

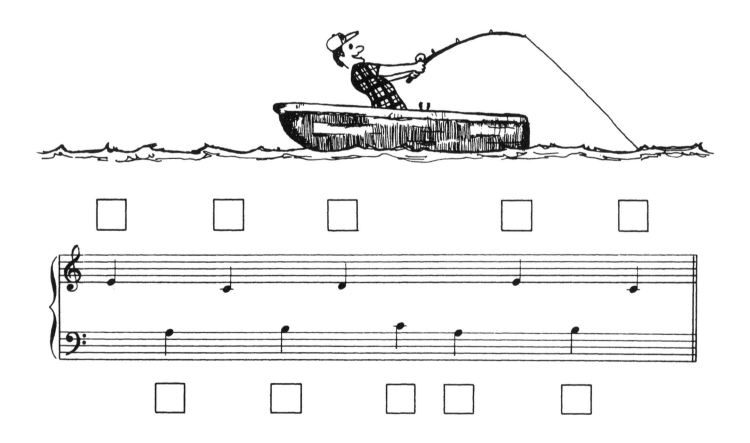

TIES

Put a **T** under each **tie** in this line of notes.

MATCH THE TIME

Draw an arrow from each group of notes to the right **time signature.**

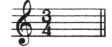

QUESTIONS

What is the letter
name of this note?

 _____

What is the letter
name of this note?

 _____

What is the name of
the sign ⌣ under
these notes?

 _____

44

A BUMPY STREET

Moderately fast
Louder on the "Bump" notes

BY EDNA MAE BURNAM

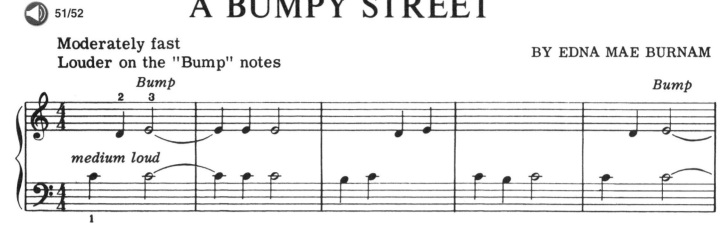

RESTS

A **rest** is a sign of silence.

A **one** count rest:

This is a **quarter** rest.

This kind of rest gets **ONE** count.

When you see a rest sign, you must lift your hand from the keyboard and count the rest.

Here is a piece that has some one count rests:

53/54

JUMP ROPE

Count   1,   2,   3,   4

Your hands do **not** always rest at the same time.
Sometimes they **take turns** resting.

Play the piece below:

HOP SCOTCH

55/56

TWO COUNT RESTS

This kind of rest gets **two** counts.

It sits on the **middle** line of each staff.

This is a **half** rest.

Here is a piece that has some two count rests.

ROCKING CHAIR

57/58

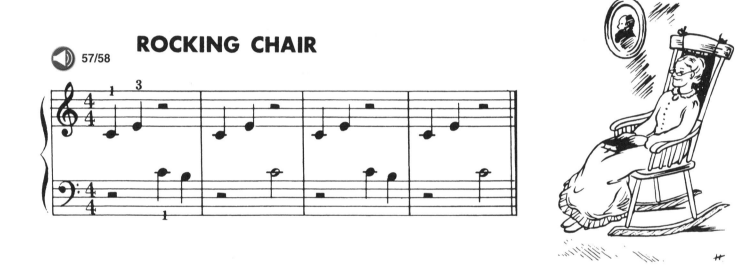

This piece has some **one** count rests and also some **two** count rests.

BUMPY STREETS

59/60

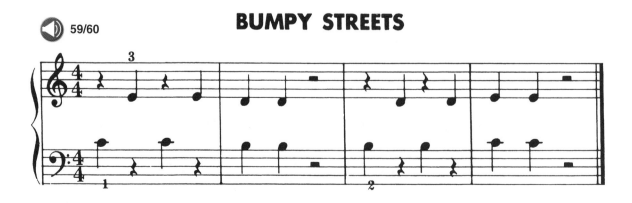

FOUR COUNT RESTS

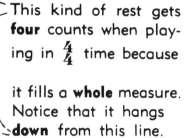

1, 2, 3, 4

This kind of rest gets **four** counts when play-ing in $\frac{4}{4}$ time because

it fills a **whole** measure. Notice that it hangs **down** from this line.

(This is a **whole** rest)

1, 2, 3

When playing in $\frac{3}{4}$ time this same kind of rest gets **three** counts because it fills the whole measure.

(Whole rest)

61/62

SHEEP

Sheep are stand-ing | on a hill, and | they stand ver-y | still.

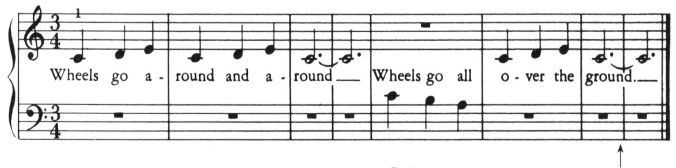

63/64

WHEELS

Wheels go a - | round and a - | round ___ | Wheels go all | o - ver the | ground.___

Did you remember to count this tie?

BABY BUGGIES

The **rest** tells how many hours the baby will nap (rest) in the baby buggy.
Draw a line from each **rest** to the baby buggy that has the right number of hours the baby will nap.

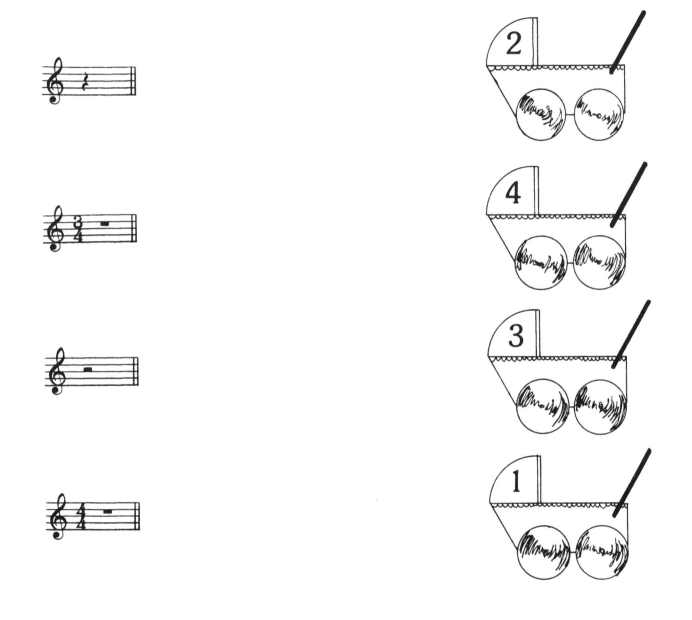

BAR LINES

This line of notes needs **bar lines.**
Draw in **bar lines** in the right places, and put a **double bar** at the end.

SALT AND PEPPER SHAKERS

There is a **note** or **rest** in every salt shaker.
Write the right number of **counts** the note or rest receives in the matching pepper shaker.

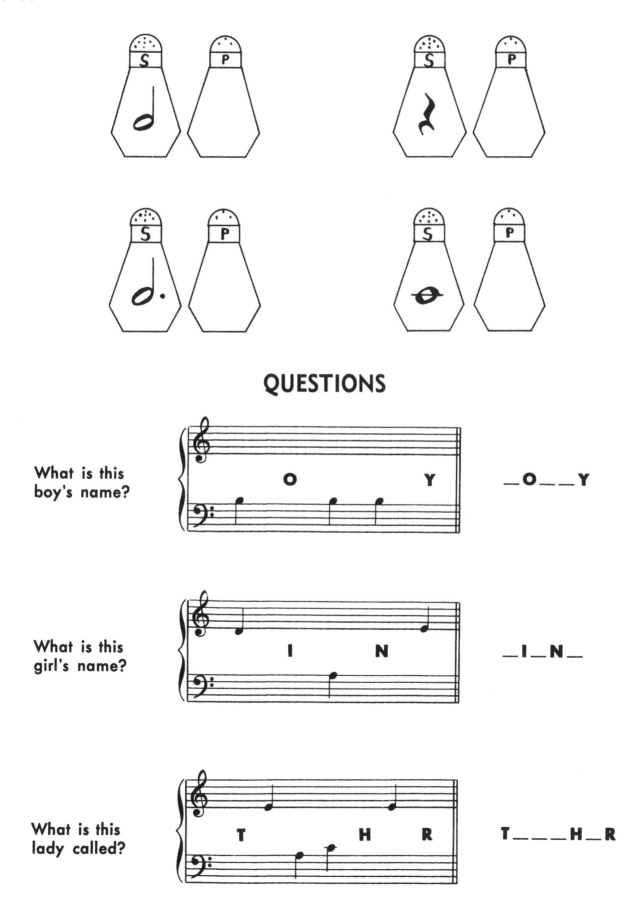

QUESTIONS

What is this boy's name?

_ O _ _ Y

What is this girl's name?

_ I _ N _

What is this lady called?

T _ _ _ _ H _ R

50

A CAMEL ON THE DESERT

65/66

BY EDNA MAE BURNAM

Moderately slow
Languid

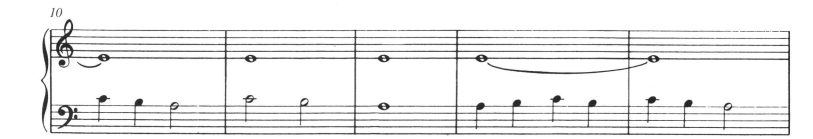

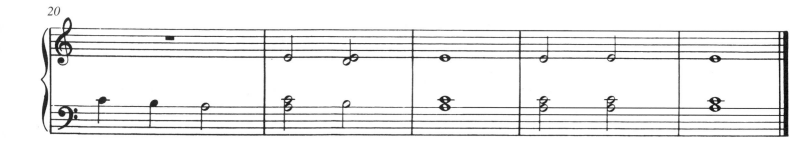

MAIL MAN

67/68

Mail - man, I'm   so   tired of   wait - ing,

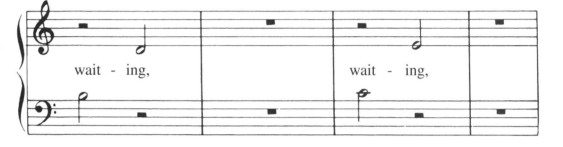

wait - ing,   wait - ing,

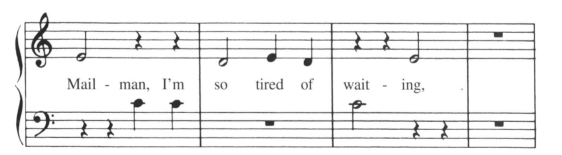

Mail - man, I'm   so   tired of   wait - ing,

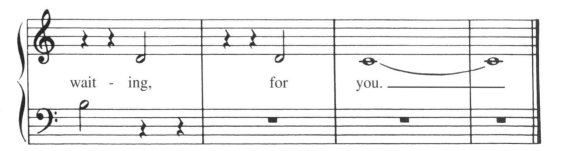

wait - ing,   for   you. _____

F ON KEYBOARD

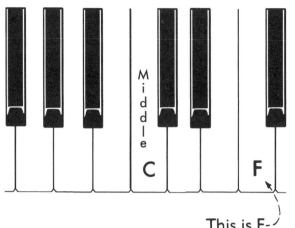

Find the white note to the **right** of E.

This is F

Here are some pictures of F.

F is **not** in MIDDLE C's play yard.

It is on the **treble** staff.

Remember that the places **between** the lines are called **spaces.**

How many spaces are on the treble staff?

F is on the treble staff and in **this** space.

Play F with the **fourth** finger of your **right** hand.

Sing F as you play it.

Here is a piece for you to play.

🔊 69/70

THE NIGHT

When I go out - side and look in - to the night,

I can see the stars, All beau - ti - ful and bright.

CORN ON THE COB

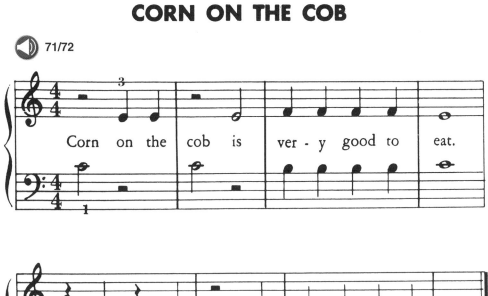

Corn on the cob is ver-y good to eat.

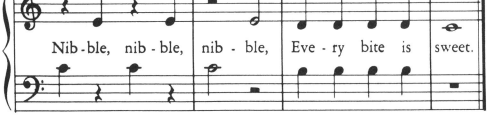

Nib-ble, nib-ble, nib-ble, Eve-ry bite is sweet.

ROCK-A-BYE DOLLY

73/74

Rock-a-bye Dol-ly, I love you true. I sure-ly hope that you love me, too!

SONG IN THE MEADOW

75/76

BY EDNA MAE BURNAM

Moderately fast
In a singing style

medium soft

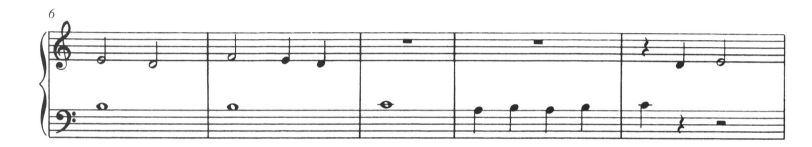

Hold these notes.

slower

DIVING FOR DIMES

Each note is a dime.
Write the letter name of each note in the box by the note.
The diver will recover every dime (note) that you write right.

WHAT'S THE TIME?

Write the right **time signature** for this line of notes.

A BAG OF GROCERIES

Write the right number of **counts** for each note or rest in the box.
This will tell you how many of each grocery item the bag contains.

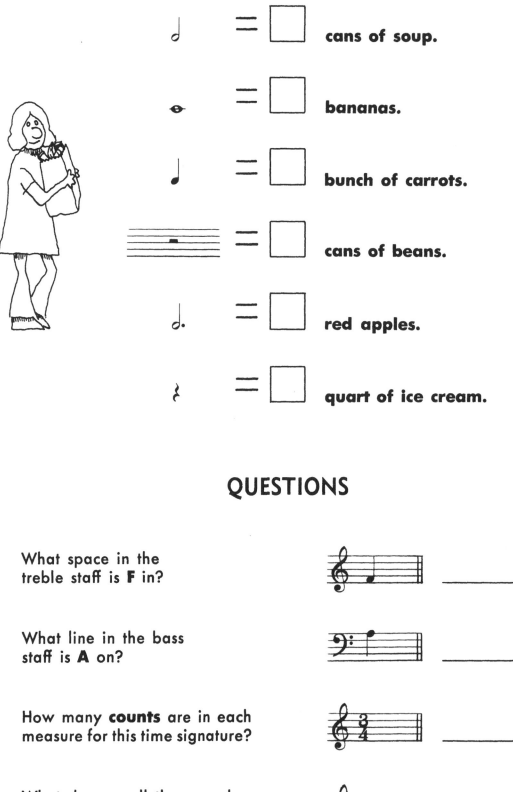

𝅗𝅥	= ☐	**cans of soup.**
𝅝	= ☐	**bananas.**
♩	= ☐	**bunch of carrots.**
▬	= ☐	**cans of beans.**
𝅗𝅥.	= ☐	**red apples.**
𝄽	= ☐	**quart of ice cream.**

QUESTIONS

What space in the
treble staff is **F** in?   _____

What line in the bass
staff is **A** on?   _____

How many **counts** are in each
measure for this time signature?   _____

What do we call the curved
line under these notes?   _____

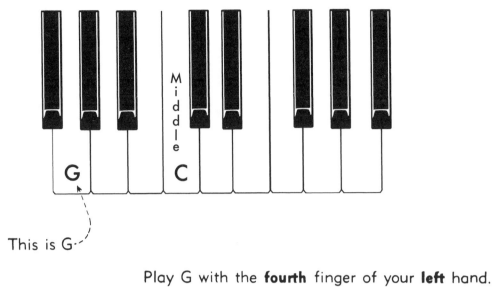

Find the
white note
to the **left**
of A.
(Below MIDDLE C)

G

C

This is G·

Play G with the **fourth** finger of your **left** hand.

Sing G as you play it.

Here are some pictures of G for the **left** hand.

This G is on the **bass** staff.

It is on **this** space of the bass staff.

LITTLE RIVER

🔊 77/78

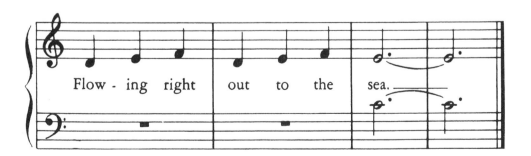

On goes the swift lit - tle riv - er,

Flow - ing right out to the sea.

EVERYBODY MARCH

79/80

BY EDNA MAE BURNAM

Play like a march.

medium loud

gradually louder – to the end

loud

EVENING

81/82

In the ear-ly eve-ning shad-ows fall.

I like ear-ly eve-ning best of all.

LONDON BRIDGE

83/84

Traditional

Lon-don bridge is fall-ing down, Fall-ing down, Fall-ing down,

Lon-don bridge is fall-ing down, My Fair Lad-y-o.

Write the right letter name on the key for every **A, B, C, D, E, F** and **G** on this keyboard.

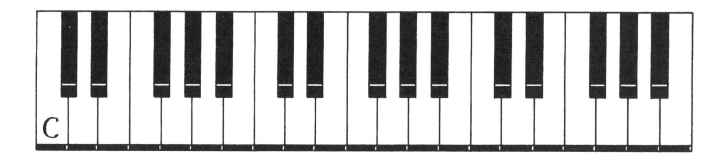

ICE CREAM WAGON

Write the letter names
of the notes the ICE CREAM
WAGON is playing.
If you write all of them
right, you will receive an
ice cream cone!

BAGS OF CANDY

The notes and rests on each bag of candy tell how many pieces of candy are inside.
Write the right number of candies (counts) in the box under each candy bag.
If you get the right number for all of them, you will receive a piece of candy!

☐   ☐   ☐   ☐

QUESTIONS

Is this **E**
a line note?

_____

Is this **G**
a line note?

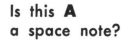

_____

Is this **F**
a space note?

_____

Is this **A**
a space note?

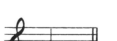

_____

G ABOVE MIDDLE C – ON KEYBOARD

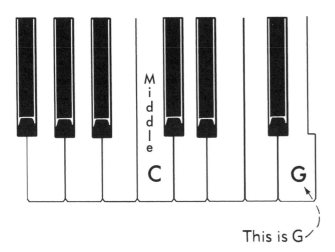

Find the white note
to the **right** of F (above Middle C).

This is G

Here are some pictures of G
for the **right** hand.

It is on **this** line of the **treble**
staff.

Play this G with the **fifth** finger of your **right** hand.

Sing G as you play it.

HILLS

85/86

Hills go up and hills go down all

in and out the cit-y. Hills go up and hills go down, and they are ver-y pret-ty.

TV ANTENNAS

87/88

T - V an - ten - nas standing in the air.

T - V an - ten - nas, Here and eve - ry - where.

MARY HAD A LITTLE LAMB

89/90

Traditional

Mar - y had a lit - tle lamb, lit - tle lamb, lit - tle lamb.

Mar - y had a lit - tle lamb, Its fleece was white as snow.

Draw a square around each **line note**.
Draw a circle around each **space note**.

BIRD NESTS

There are some bird eggs in each nest.
The **notes** and **rests** under each nest tell how many eggs are in each nest.
Write the right number of eggs **(counts)** in the box under each nest.

A SENTENCE

Write the **right letter** names to complete this sentence.

IS   R   T   O Y.

_ _   IS   _   _R_ _T   _O Y.

QUESTIONS

How many lines are in
the treble staff?   _____

How many spaces are in
the treble staff?   _____

How many lines are in
the bass staff?   _____

How many spaces are in
the bass staff?   _____

TWO CHILDREN HUMMING

91/92

Lit - tle chil - dren hum - ming, hum - ming, hum - ming,

Lit - tle chil - dren hum - ming, all day long.

SUNSET

93/94

When the sun sets way down low,

Beau - ti - ful and bright. When the sun sets then I know, It is near - ly night.

FISHING

Draw a fishing line from each pole to the fish it should catch.

If the pole is marked C, the line must go to the note C.

If you get it right, it means you caught the fish!

See how many fish (notes) you can catch.

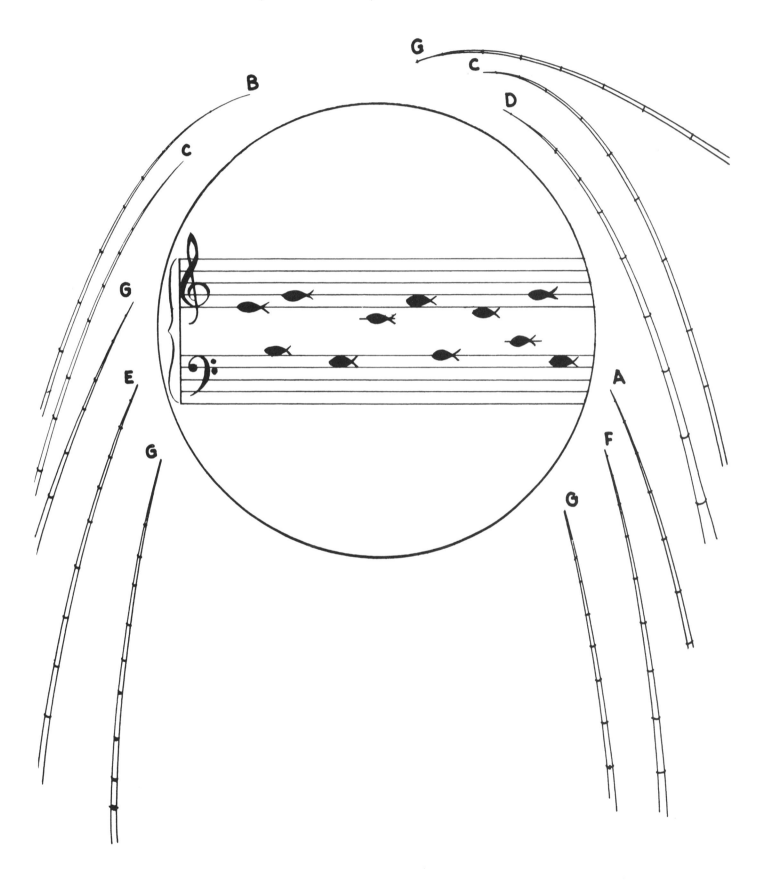

Write the letter names of the **musical alphabet** in the center boxes below.

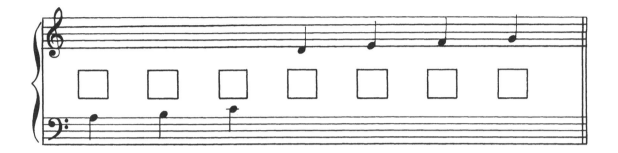

Write the letter names of the musical alphabet **backwards** in the center boxes below.

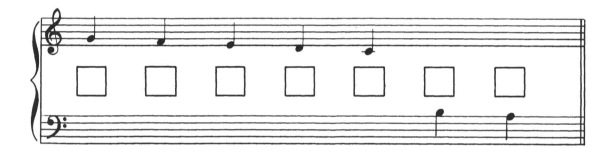

METRONOME TICKS

Write the right **time signature** for this line of metronome ticks.

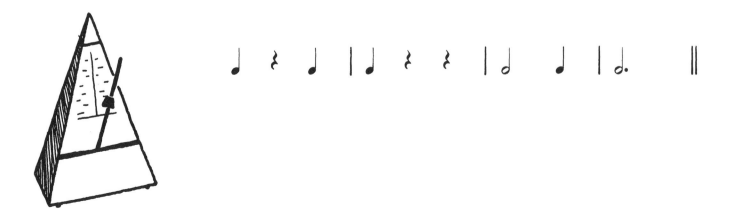

WHIZ QUIZ

Write the right answer in each of the boxes.

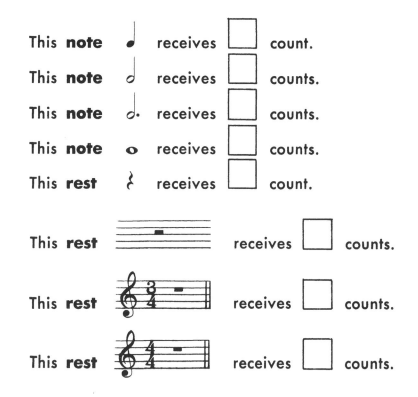

This **note** ♩ receives ☐ count.

This **note** 𝅗𝅥 receives ☐ counts.

This **note** 𝅗𝅥· receives ☐ counts.

This **note** 𝅝 receives ☐ counts.

This **rest** 𝄿 receives ☐ count.

This **rest** ▬ receives ☐ counts.

This **rest** (3/4) ▬ receives ☐ counts.

This **rest** (4/4) ▬ receives ☐ counts.

Draw a line from the terms on the left to the matching music notation signs on the right.

Treble clef

Bass clef

Bar line

Measure

Time signature

Double bar

Tie

QUESTIONS

How many letters are there in the **Music Alphabet?** _____

What are the names of the letters in the Music Alphabet? _____

What are the names of the letters in the
Music Alphabet **backwards?** _____

PENNIES IN A PURSE

Each purse has pennies inside it.

How many pennies are there in each purse?

There are as many pennies as there are counts in the notes.

Write the number of counts in each purse.

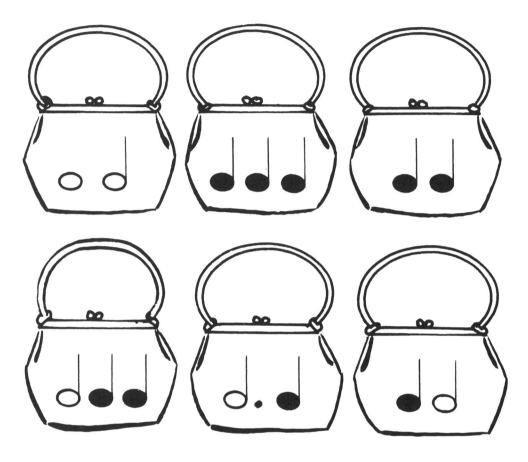

This time count the **notes and rests.**

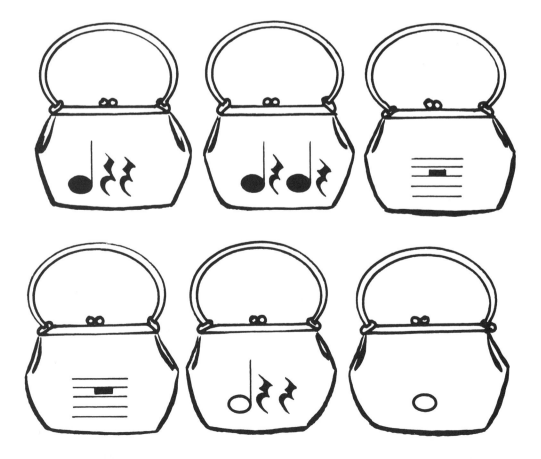

DUCKS

Each duck quacks four measures.

They quack in either **2/4** , **3/4** or **4/4** time.

Write the correct time signature before each line.

Then write the counts under the notes or rests.

Like this:

72

LITTLE WHITE CHICKENS

Lit - tle white chick - ens in Grand - moth - er's yard,

All the day long they keep peck - ing ver - y hard.

SOUTH WIND

97/98

High up in the tall - est tree,

Oo - - - - oo, South wind sings a song to me, Oo - - - - oo.

HIGHWAYS

High-ways go just eve-ry-where, On hills and des-erts, too.

Coun-tries, cit-ies, eve-ry-where, and by the sea so blue.

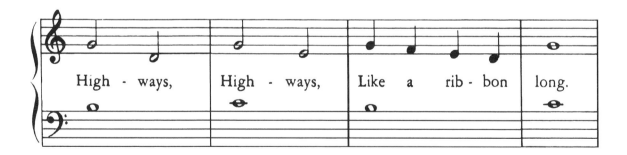

High-ways, High-ways, Like a rib-bon long.

High-ways, High-ways, Beau-ti-ful and strong.

BEACH BALL BOUNCE

101/102

BY EDNA MAE BURNAM

Bouncy and happy

medium loud

slower to the end

FINAL CHECK-UP

Your teacher will give you this final check-up.

- Tell me how your fingers are numbered for playing the piano.

- Show me a:

  Treble clef
  Bass clef
  Grand staff
  Bar line
  Measure
  Double bar
  Brace
  Time Signature

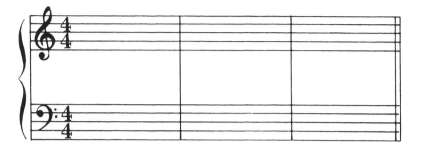

- Show me a note that gets:

  1 count
  2 counts
  3 counts
  4 counts

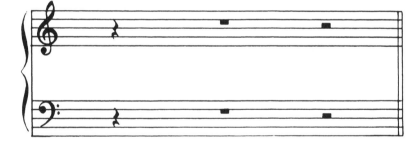

- Show me a rest that gets:

  1 count
  2 counts
  4 counts

- Show me a time signature that means:

  2 counts to each measure
  4 counts to each measure
  3 counts to each measure

- Show me a tie:

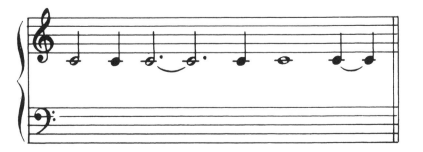

Certificate of Merit

This certifies that

....

has successfully completed

BOOK ONE
OF
EDNA MAE BURNAM'S
PIANO COURSE

STEP BY STEP

and is eligible for promotion to

BOOK TWO

....
Teacher

....
Date

Edna Mae Burnam was a pioneer in piano publishing. The creator of the iconic *A Dozen a Day* technique series and *Step by Step* method was born on September 15, 1907 in Sacramento, California. She began lessons with her mother, a piano teacher who drove a horse and buggy daily through the Sutter Buttes mountain range to reach her students. In college Burnam decided that she too enjoyed teaching young children, and majored in elementary education at California State University (then Chico State College) with a minor in music. She spent several years teaching kindergarten in public schools before starting her own piano studio and raising daughters Pat and Peggy. She delighted in composing for her students, and took theory and harmony lessons from her husband David (a music professor and conductor of the Sacramento Symphony in the 1940s).

Burnam began submitting original pieces to publishers in the mid-1930s, and was thrilled when one of them, "The Clock That Stopped," was accepted, even though her remuneration was a mere $20. Undaunted, the industrious composer sent in the first *A Dozen a Day* manuscript to her Willis editor in 1950, complete with stick-figure sketches for each exercise. Her editor loved the simple genius of the playful artwork resembling a musical technique, and so did students and teachers: the book rapidly blossomed into a series of seven and continues to sell millions of copies. In 1959, the first book in the *Step by Step* series was published, with hundreds of individual songs and pieces along the way, often identified by whimsical titles in Burnam's trademark style.

The immense popularity of her books solidified Edna Mae Burnam's place and reputation in music publishing history, yet throughout her lifetime she remained humble and effervescent. "I always left our conversations feeling upbeat and happy," says Kevin Cranley, Willis president. "She could charm the legs off a piano bench," Bob Sylva of the *Sacramento Bee* wrote, "make a melody out of a soap bubble, and a song out of a moon beam."

Burnam died in 2007, a few months shy of her 100th birthday. "Music enriches anybody's life, even if you don't turn out to be musical," she said once in an interview. "I can't imagine being in a house without a piano."

STEP INTO SUCCESS...
with Step by Step!

By Edna Mae Burnam

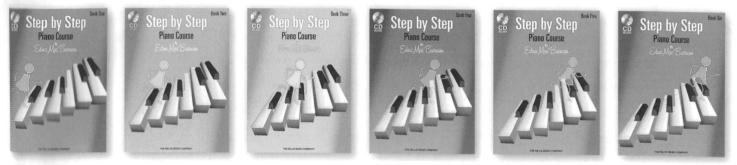

The *Step by Step Piano Course* provides students with an opportunity to learn the piano in a unique and charming way, with each lesson presented in a logical order and at a manageable pace.

METHOD BOOKS

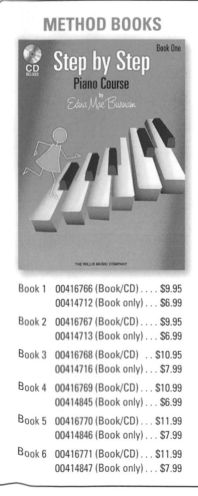

Book 1	00416766 (Book/CD)	$9.95
	00414712 (Book only) . . .	$6.99
Book 2	00416767 (Book/CD)	$9.95
	00414713 (Book only) . . .	$6.99
Book 3	00416768 (Book/CD) . .	$10.95
	00414716 (Book only) . . .	$7.99
Book 4	00416769 (Book/CD) . . .	$10.99
	00414845 (Book only) . . .	$6.99
Book 5	00416770 (Book/CD) . . .	$11.99
	00414846 (Book only) . . .	$7.99
Book 6	00416771 (Book/CD) . . .	$11.99
	00414847 (Book only) . . .	$7.99

SOLO BOOKS

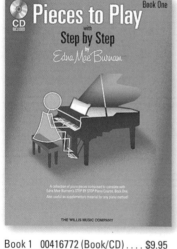

Book 1	00416772 (Book/CD)	$9.95
	00404507 (Book only) . . .	$5.99
Book 2	00416773 (Book/CD)	$9.95
	00404508 (Book only) . . .	$5.99
Book 3	00416774 (Book/CD)	$9.95
	00404550 (Book only) . . .	$5.99
Book 4	00416775 (Book/CD)	$9.95
	00404567 (Book only) . . .	$5.99
Book 5	00416776 (Book/CD)	$9.99
	00404604 (Book only) . . .	$5.99
Book 6	00416777 (Book/CD)	$9.99
	00404627 (Book only) . . .	$5.99

THEORY BOOKS

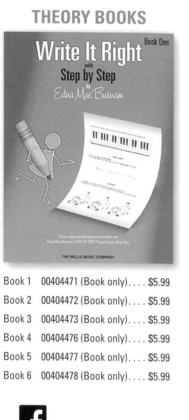

Book 1	00404471 (Book only)	$5.99
Book 2	00404472 (Book only)	$5.99
Book 3	00404473 (Book only)	$5.99
Book 4	00404476 (Book only)	$5.99
Book 5	00404477 (Book only)	$5.99
Book 6	00404478 (Book only)	$5.99

f willispianomusic

www.willispianomusic.com

WILLIS MUSIC

EXCLUSIVELY DISTRIBUTED BY
HAL•LEONARD®